Livewire

John Travolta

Julia Holt

JAMESTOWN PUBLISHERS

a division of NTC/CONTEMPORARY PUBLISHING GROUP
Lincolnwood, Illinois USA

Acknowledgments
Cover photo:
© MGM/Shooting Star

Photos:
Page 3 © S.S./Shooting Star
Page 6 & 14 © Tri–Star Pictures/Shooting Star
Page 11 © S.S. Archives/Shooting Star
Page 17 © Ron Davis/Shooting Star Int'l
Page 20 © Miramax Films/Shooting Star
Page 23 © MGM/Shooting Star
Page 25 © 20th Century Fox/Shooting Star Int'l

First published in United Kingdom by Hodder & Stoughton
Educational in Association with the Basic Skills Agency.

ISBN: 0-89061-423-7

Published by Jamestown Publishers,
a division of NTC/Contemporary Publishing Group, Inc.
4255 West Touhy Avenue,
Lincolnwood (Chicago), Illinois 60646–1975 U.S.A.
© 1998 by NTC/Contemporary Publishing Group, Inc.

890 V P 0 9 8 7 6 5 4 3 2 1

REAL LIVES

John Travolta

Contents

Beginning

John Travolta
has been a star twice.
In 1977
he was the king of disco dancing.
Not many actors
could get rid of a label like that.

Now he is a star again.
A film star.
How has he done it?

John knew
he was going to be an actor.
Everybody knew
he was going to be an actor.

His mother taught acting.
She was 43
when she had her sixth child,
John Travolta.

There were no other children to play with
because his brothers and sisters were
much older than John.
So John went everywhere
with his mother.
He went with her to acting classes.

He spent hours dressing up
and tap dancing.
The little boy said,
"I want to be a star
when I grow up."

John was the baby
in his family.
He ate what he wanted
and went to bed late.
These two habits
gave him problems later in life.

It was John's dancing that made him the star of *Saturday Night Fever* many years later.

By the time he was nine,
his three older sisters
were actresses.
Many times he went to the airport
to see them fly off
for acting jobs.

That was the start
of the *second* love of his life.
A love of airplanes and flying.

He filled his bedroom
with toy planes
and books about flying.
But the first love of his life was dancing.

John did not fit in
at school in New York.
He was not like
the other kids.
Dancing helped him
to make friends.
He and his older brother
could do all the latest dances.

At the age of 16, John left school
to work as an actor.

He got work on the stage
and in TV commercials.
With the money he got
from a Pepsi commercial,
he took flying lessons.

He was paid $600 a week
for a big part
in the stage play of *Grease*.
He was still
only in his teens.

Hollywood was the next stop for John.
He had work,
but he became lonely
and had problems sleeping.

He joined The Church of Scientology.
Scientology is still an important part
of John's life today.

John has always loved flying. *In Look Who's Talking Now* he played a pilot and later in *Broken Arrow* he flew most of the planes himself.

TV Star

In 1975 a brand new TV show
started in the United States.
John played
the leader of a street gang.
He was in this show
for three years
making films at the same time.

The TV show
made John a star in America.
He was getting
ten thousand letters a week
from young fans.

He made two records,
and they sold like hotcakes.
Critics said
his records only sold
because he was a TV star.
John was not happy about this.

John had a small part
in the horror film *Carrie*.
He saved all the money he made.
But he did splurge
on an old Thunderbird car,
and his first plane.

In 1976 John fell in love with Diana.
They worked together
on a TV film.
She played his mother.
She was 19 years older than him.

What would his young fans think?

John and Diana didn't care,
because there was
a bigger problem.
Diana had cancer.

She died seven months later
in John's arms.

Film Star

John felt very low,
but he had to keep working.
He had the star part
in *Saturday Night Fever.*

The film is about young people
who spend all week
in dull jobs.
On Saturday nights
they go disco dancing.

John played Tony,
the best dancer in town.

He chose his own clothes
and made changes
to the story.
He had his own way,
and the film was a big success.
It made $350 million.

This was the start
of Travolta fever.
His clothes from the film
were sold for $2,000.

After *Saturday Night Fever*
John went back to his TV show.
He needed
to get over Diana's death.
He needed a rest,
but he didn't get one.
They started to make the film of *Grease*.
This film was made
at top speed
to fit in with John's TV show.

Grease made almost as much money
as *Saturday Night Fever.*
John said,
"Now I can do the parts I want."

But there were more problems on the way.

John dancing with Olivia Newton-John in *Grease*.

Problems

John's mother died from cancer in 1978,
just 18 months after Diana.

He was lonely
and eating too much chocolate.
He was getting fat.

Some people were not kind.
They didn't like his success.

John moved to a house
far away from others.
He locked the gates.
He needed to think about his life.
The newspapers said,
"John Travolta is finished."

From 1980 to 1988
his films did not make money.
He turned down films that did,
like *Top Gun, Splash,*
and *Scarface.*

He also turned down a part in
Interview with the Vampire.
That film wasn't made
until 16 years later,
and Tom Cruise was the star.

John still made money
from commercials made in Japan.
He got a new jet plane.
He even thought
of getting a job as a pilot
to get away from acting,
but he kept going
as an actor.

A shot from *Look Who's Talking*.

Along came a part in the film
Look Who's Talking.

There were two stars in the film.
John starred with Kirstie Alley.
John played a taxi driver.
Kirstie was his girlfriend,
and she had a talking baby.

To everyone's surprise,
Look Who's Talking was a hit.
It was filmed for $8 million,
but it made $133 million.

John went on to make
two more talking baby films.

A New Family

John moved to a new house in Florida
with a landing strip
for his plane.

He also had
a new love in his life;
a young actress called Kelly.

In 1991 John and Kelly
were married in France
by a minister
from the Church of Scientology.

In April the next year
Kelly gave birth to a son, Jett.

John with his wife, Kelly. They have a son, Jett, who was born in 1992.

In 1992 John got a call
from Quentin Tarantino,
who had just finished
writing a film
called *Pulp Fiction*.

Tarantino did not want John
to be in the film.
He wanted to meet John
because he was a fan.

He wanted to find out
what John had done
with his talents.

At first John was upset.
But then he said,
"I must have been a good actor."

But had he lost his talent?

John Is Back

A few months later,
Tarantino asked John
to be in *Pulp Fiction* after all.

Now he could show
he still had talent.
He wanted to get fit
for the film.
Tarantino said, "No."
He said John looked perfect
for the part of a middle-aged hitman
who liked drugs and French fries.

John and Quentin Tarantino in *Pulp Fiction*.

Pulp Fiction is a violent film,
but it's funny
at the same time.

It's the story
of the lives of two hitmen,
the sexy wife of their boss,
and a boxer and a drug dealer.

In 1994 it was the film
everyone talked about.
John Travolta was back.
He didn't look the same,
but he was a big star again.

His next big film
was a comedy called *Get Shorty*.
Everyone said
he was perfect for the part.
He played a small-time crook
who gets mixed up
in the film world.

He was paid $5 million
for *Get Shorty*.
With every film
his pay went up and up.

John played alongside Rene Russo, Gene Hackman, and Danny DeVito in *Get Shorty*.

Worldwide Star

In 1996 he played a crazy pilot
in *Broken Arrow*.
John got to fly
most of the planes in the film.
By now he is licensed
to fly seven different
kinds of jet planes.

In the same year
he made two films
about special powers.

The first was called *Phenomenon*.
John plays a man
who is struck
by a light from heaven.
Instantly he is winning at chess,
reading four books a day,
and learning new languages.

John said,
"I want to be this guy."

John played a crazy pilot in *Broken Arrow*.

In the second film,
Michael, he plays an angel.
He comes to earth
to help two people
put their lives back together.

The angel
also plans to enjoy his time on earth
with food, beer, and women.

Now John Travolta's comeback
is complete.

One of the three films
he made in 1997
was *Mad City.*
John plays a museum guard
who gets fired.
He takes a lot of people
hostage in the museum.
Dustin Hoffman plays the
TV news reporter
who has to sort it out.

In 1998
John played the United States President.
The film is called *Primary Colors*.
It's about the Presidential election of 1992.
Tom Hanks turned the part down
and John took it.
He watched videos
of Bill Clinton
to get ready for the film.

John Travolta is a worldwide star again.

People go to see John Travolta films
just because he is in them.

One thing shows John is a star.

His clothes from *Saturday Night Fever*
have been sold again.

This time for $145,500!